WHISTLER · GARIBALDI
SEA to SKY

JOSEF HANUS & JOSEF M. HANUS

Personal gift to:

....

From:

DOROTHY SWANSON
ROYAL LEPAGE
BLACK TUSK REALTY
BOX 640
GARIBALDI HIGHLANDS, B.C. V0N 1T0
PHONE: (604) 898-5904
....

Georgia Strait

Cotton-candy clouds linger over the reflective surface of the Georgia Strait. Stretching 240 kilometres from the intersection of Puget Sound and the Strait of Juan de Fuca to Johnson Strait, the Strait of Georgia separates Vancouver Island from the mainland of British Columbia. A major navigation channel in North America, the strait is often busy with water traffic maneuvering around its many islands to deliver people and goods to the many ports along its shores.

Inside Passage

The beginning of the Sea to Sky Highway in West Vancouver is also the gate of the Inside Passage Route. Countless cruise ships ply the waters of the 500 kilometre-long route which officially stretches from Port Hardy to Prince Rupert.

2

Cypress Bowl

Vancouver has several of Canada's best skiing areas. The most popular of Vancouver's mountains is Cypress Bowl, located just 30 minutes from downtown. Excellent terrain for both downhill and cross-country skiing is open to the public, day and night from early December into the spring. In summer months, hikers and mountain bikers occupy the mountains and hills above the metropolis.

Point Atkinson

From the rocky shores of the western edge of West Vancouver the beacon of the Point Atkinson Lighthouse illuminates the waters of the Georgia Strait. The original construction of the lighthouse in 1875 was replaced with today's hexagonal reinforced concrete structure in 1912. 75 hectares of the lush rainforest of Lighthouse Park surrounds the lighthouse.

3

West Vancouver

The Lions

The Coast Mountains form a dramatic backdrop to the city of Vancouver, stretching from Howe Sound to Indian Arm and reaching heights of over 1,500 metres. The twin peaks of 'The Lions' are a well known part of the mountains, standing stoic as docile guardians of the city. The peaks were named for their resemblance to the Landseer Lions in London's Trafalgar Square.

Grouse Mountain

In addition to Cypress Bowl and Mount Seymour, Grouse Mountain offers some of the best views of Greater Vancouver. Grouse Mountain can be easily reached from downtown via public transit and the Skyride Gondola, or, for the more adventurous, via the Grouse Grind hiking trail, or the Old Grouse Mountain Highway.

4

Mount Ellesmere

Heading from Horseshoe Bay to the Langdale Terminal near the town of Gibsons, the 'Queen of Surrey' has served BC Ferries since 1981, connecting the Sunshine Coast with the mainland with sixteen daily trips. Mount Ellesmere can be seen left of centre within the peaks rising up from the glorious, empyreal clouds above the Queen Charlotte Channel.

Mount Seymour

Vancouver's third local ski area is Mount Seymour Provincial Park, reaching up into the eastern edge of North Vancouver's rugged mountains and offering family friendly slopes with fine skiing and snowboarding for beginners and experienced alike.

5

Coast Mountains

Vancouver Beaches

Within the jungle of apartment buildings that give the city its distinctive skyline, West End is Canada's most urban and most densely populated area per square kilometre, stretching west from Burrard Street to Stanley Park. Several kilometers of sunny sandy beaches stretch from Yaletown to Third Beach, the sea air offering a revitalizing kick to the environment along and around West End.

The Timer

To help Vancouverites count down to the start of the Olympic Winter Games on February 12, 2010, the Swiss Omega watch company unveiled the 'Vancouver 2010 Countdown Clock', on February 12, 2007. The huge electronic clock tick-tocks in anticipation at the Vancouver Art Gallery on West Georgia Street.

False Creek

The land around False Creek and Granville Island remained intensely industrial until the 1950s, playing host to sawmills, small port operations, and the western terminus of the major Canadian railways. Though the area experienced economic decline as industry began to modernize, it received a breath of new life in the 1970s with the development of several exclusive residential neighbourhoods.

BC Place Stadium

The world's largest air-supported domed stadium was constructed for the 1986 World Exposition on Transportation and Communication, also known as Expo '86. With the capacity to hold 60,000 people, BC Place Stadium will host the 2010 Winter Olympic Games Opening and Closing ceremonies.

7

Vancouver

Stanley Park Totems

Totem poles in Brockton Point in Stanley Park include a house post, a memorial pole and a mortuary pole. Some of the most common animals carved on totem poles are bears, wolves, ravens, eagles, frogs, killer whales and hawks. Mythical beings also have their place on the sculptures, however totem poles are not religious icons but rather celebrations of culture.

Horseshoe Bay

Driving north to Squamish and Whistler, the last possible pit-stop in West Vancouver is Horseshoe Bay, also the BC Ferries port which connects Vancouver to Vancouver Island and the Sunshine Coast.

8

Greater Vancouver

Howe Sound

Howe Sound, home to North America's southernmost fjord and a popular playground of Vancouverites, brings the Pacific Ocean in to the Squamish Valley. Several communities near Howe Sound, which is actually a triangular network of several fjords, boast some of the finest and most expensive waterfront homes in British Columbia.

Ansell Place

A new neighbour of Horseshoe Bay, Ansell Place attracts its residents with its panoramic views of the Queen Charlotte Channel. Ansell Place is located just above the Sea to Sky Highway, Strachan Creek is close to Lions Bay and Sunset Beach is just below by the coast.

Howe Sound

Furry Creek

The shores of Howe Sound play host to Furry Creek, a 1,036 acre planned community known for its country club and exquisitely landscaped golf course. A steep ascent of the new highway cuts through the hills of Furry Creek.

The smaller picture shows the famous Furry Crek Golf Course.

10

Lions Bay

Close to Horseshoe Bay in West Vancouver, Lions Bay is located above and below the Sea to Sky Highway. A popular residential area sits partially above the highway amidst forest on steep topography, while other homes can be found closer to the ocean and a popular small town beach, resulting in roughly 1300 residents.

Harvey Creek

To the right, a Highway #99 bridge crossing Harvey Creek with the expanse of Howe Sound and Gambier Island in the background.

11

Lions Bay

Britannia Beach

Located on the Howe Sound halfway between Vancouver and the world class ski resort of Whistler, Britannia Beach is a popular stop on the Sea to Sky Highway. This picture was taken from The CRS Trading Post, which carries a variety of unique local Native American carvings, jewelry, artwork, BC Jade and other souvenirs. Nestled under the Britannia Mountains in the Squamish-Lillooet Regional Area, the small community's history dates back to 1859, when hydrographer Captain Richards came to the area, naming it after the 100 gun frigate HMS Britannia. Several improvements are in the works for the highway running through the area as well as the waterfront in time for the 2010 Olympic Games.

On the opposite page, weekenders enjoying the rushing waters of Britannia Creek.

12

BC Museum of Mining

Wandering through the historic area of Britannia Beach, you can enjoy a snack or cappuccino and visit the BC Museum of Mining-the site of the mine which, until 1974, was responsible for the largest production of copper in the British Empire. After the copper mines were discovered by Dr. A. A. Forbes in 1888, Britannia was a working mining town until the ore reserves ran out in the early 1970s. Since 1975, the BC Mining Museum has been open to the public and in 2005 the museum was rebuilt to its current impressive condition. In 1988 the museum was designated as a National Historic Site and in 1989 was named a British Columbia Historic Landmark.

13

Britannia Beach

Minaty Bay

Minaty Bay is a romantic little offshoot of Howe Sound, not far from Furry Creek. Numerous waterfront accesses along the rocky beach, a playing field and a perfectly positioned viewpoint of layered folds of mountains pull in many visitors to the newly developed Minaty Park.

Brunswick Beach

This part of Howe Sound is called Brunswick Beach, and is located just under the segment of highway pictured here. Gambier Island, Howe Sound's largest island, can be seen in the background.

14

Furry Creek

Porteau Cove

Porteau Cove Provincial Park, spanning 50 hectares, features a picnic area, a fully serviced campground situated right on the ocean shore and a boat launch. Artificial reefs and access to two sunken vessels make Porteau Cove popular with scuba divers, and several, easily accessible dive sites can be found within the park. Porteau Cove is also among the most popular windsurfing spots in British Columbia, along with Alice Lake and Britannia Beach.

Oliver's Landing

Oliver's Landing, in Furry Creek, is a charming community which offers beachfront homes on its lower level as well as ocean view homes in its 'Uplands,' above the Sea to Sky Highway.

15

Porteau Cove

Sea to Sky

The grandiose beauty of the incredibly scenic section of Highway #99 which runs from Horseshoe Bay in West Vancouver to Lillooet, commonly referred to as the Sea to Sky Highway, stuns travelers so that its 310 kilometres pass by in a mere blink. Best known as the Vancouver/Whistler connector, the Sea to Sky Highway passes through some of British Columbia's most picturesque and thrilling places, including Squamish, Lillooet, Pemberton and, of course, Vancouver and Whistler.

The larger picture was taken from the first peak of Stawamus Chief, often dubbed 'The Chief,' showing the highway as it snakes alongside Darrell Bay. The smaller photo shows the newly constructed Ansell Place Underpass, built as part of the Sea to Sky Highway Improvement Project.

16

Browning Lake

A small but very popular family weekend destination is Browning Lake. Located near Squamish in Murrin Provincial Park, the lake is ideal for swimming and trout fishing. Several quaint picnic areas can be found throughout the park and hiking trails weave in and out of untouched natural settings.

Darrell Bay

A shot of Howe Sound, with Darrell Bay on its left. The old ferry port, which once provided connections to Woodfibre, Mount Ellesmere and Sechelet Ridge, is visible just left of center next to the highway.

17

Murrin Park

Squamish Nation

Squamish Nation refers to an Indian Act imposed upon indigenous tribes by the Canadian government in the late 19th century. The 'Nation' is actually a composite of several different but related villages forced onto reservations by the act. The cultural centre for many of the villages is a longhouse. A small portion of a Coast Salish longhouse located directly beneath Stawamus Chief, is pictured here behind the traditional wood carving.

Living in Squamish

The mountainous community of Squamish, surrounded by the dramatic Coast Range Mountains, is spread throughout the mouth of the Squamish River and its surrounding hills. This beautifully settled part of the city, is located on the cliffs just above the highway.

18

Smoke Bluffs

Mount Garibaldi, Smoke Bluffs, The Chief's Second Peak and Brackendale Eagles Provincial Park can be observed from The Chief's First Peak. Smoke Bluffs, craggy, spattered with pine, is pictured here.

Peaks of Stawamus Chief

Each of the three peaks of the granite dome Stawamus Chief offers glorious views of Howe Sound. First Peak, also known as South Summit, stands at 610 metres; Second Peak, or Centre Summit, at 655 metres; and Third Peak, or North Summit, at 702 metres. The Squamish people indigenous to this region believe the Chief to have spiritual significance.

Squamish

Stawamus Chief

A popular challenge for rock climbers, the Stawamus Chief, reaching seven hundred metres with its North Summit, is 93 million years old. Though many people assert the massif to be the second largest granite monolith in the world, it is actually much smaller than granite formations on Baffin Island, in Pakistan, and in Yosemite Valley.

Squamish Spit

The Squamish Spit, located at the mouth of the Squamish River, has been popular with windsurfers since 1980. Afternoon winds are accelerated by warm air from Howe Sound to a speed of some 20–25 knots. The sport has become so popular in the area that a non-profit windsurfing society was established in Squamish in 1988.

20

Port of Squamish

Trans-oceanic ships of all sizes can reach Squamish via North America's deepest and southernmost fjord - Howe Sound. The sea-port terminal, Port of Squamish, is located in the northern part of Howe Sound near the town of Squamish. Redesigned as a public harbour in 1988, the port is also home to hundreds of private and commercial vessels.

Howe Sound History

In 1791, the first European explorer to chart the region, Spanish navigator Jose Maria Narvaez, named Howe Sound 'Boca del Carmelo'. One year later Englishman George Vancouver re-named it after Earl Howe. These early European explorers were first greeted by the indigenous Squamish people who had wandered throughout the region for thousands of years and established settlements along the sound's shores.

21

Squamish

Goat Ridge

Mount Habrich is located high above Shannon Falls in the Goat Ridge.

Spring Hiking

Garibaldi Provincial Park remains one of the most popular hiking destinations in the province. This picture was taken from Diamond Head Trail in Paul Ridge. The trail starts high above the residential neighbourhood of Garibaldi Estates and leads to Garibaldi Lake and the smaller Mamquam Lake. Experienced hikers can continue along the more rugged path to Black Tusk. Shelters can be found along the trail for those who want to spend a night or two in the park, which I would definitely recommend-no one can imagine the spectacular sight of the night sky from 2,500 metres without having seen it in person!

22

Sky Pilot

A view from Clinker Ridge beautifully shows Goat Ridge with the dominant Sky Pilot Mountain at 2,031 metres in the centre. On the left is Mount Habrich at 1,792 metres. Even though the distance between these mountains is some three kilometres and Mount Habrich is closer to the camera, the telephoto lens effect makes them seem almost at the same level.

Cheakamus Lake

An aerial picture of the reflective waters of Cheakamus Lake, resting peacefully in the centre of the Fitzsimmons Range. The lake can be reached by the short 3.5 kilometre Cheakamus Lake Trail. Near the lake, in the nearby dense forest, are two wilderness camping areas. The highest peak above the lake is Mount Davidson at 2,516 metres.

Garibaldi Park

Ashlu Creek

Hidden in Ashlu Creek Valley, Ashlu Creek empties into the Squamish River. There are numerous popular camping places scattered along the banks of the creek. The structure of the area was recently altered by the Ashlu Creek Green Power Project, which produces electricity from the creek's naturally flowing water.

Cheakamus River

This dramatic picture of the Cheakamus River was taken from the trail to Black Tusk. Wild emerald waters bursting forth from the river in spring attract whitewater rafters and kayakers. The river, beginning in Garibaldi Park, drains melted mountain snow and joins the Squamish River at Cheekye.

24

Squamish Valley

Shannon Falls

Standing 330 metres above Highway #99, Shannon Falls are the third highest falls in the province. The water source originates in the granite horn Mount Habrich. Almost half a million visitors annually stop in the park on the way north to Whistler and Pemberton.

Elaho River

A tributary of the Squamish River, the Elaho River begins in the Coast Mountains. Whitewater rafting is a popular draw of both rivers, thanks to the views of glaciers, waterfalls, hidden mountain peaks and wildlife, which can only be seen from the water. The Upper Elaho River's intense scenery can offer new sensations to even the most experienced boaters.

25

Shannon Falls

Squamish

Before Captain George Vancouver made contact with indigenous people in 1792 near Brackendale, the Squamish Valley area was inhabited by the Squohomish tribes, who lived, hunted and fished in North Vancouver and Squamish Valley. This picture shows the Mamquam Blind Channel, Port of Squamish and downtown Squamish, framed by the mountains and surrounding hills which make up the area known as the Squamish Valley. This West Coast community dating back to 1889 is home to some 17,000 residents. Forestry is the area's main industry, next to tourism and service. It is not uncommon that Vancouver residents escape to the valley from the city due to rising living costs. This growth has led to the opening of numerous big-city stores, meaning all the services of Vancouver can now be found locally.

26

Squamish

Whistler Mountaineer

A most dramatic scenic trip can be taken on the Whistler Mountaineer train from North Vancouver to Whistler. Passengers can choose from one-day trips or adventurous multi-day trips which offer a more thorough look at Whistler and the surrounding areas. Trips are usually scheduled from May to October.

Royal Hudson

Displayed now in the West Coast Railway Heritage Park in Squamish, the famous locomotive of Royal Hudson No. 2860 served an excursion service from 1973 to 2001 between North Vancouver and Squamish. This popular BC tourist attraction carried some 145,000 passengers per season. Occasionally, the Royal Hudson still operates under her own steam power for special occasions.

27

Squamish

Brackendale Eagles

Brackendale is a residential community north of Squamish, which every winter becomes a meeting place for three to four thousands bald eagles, feeding on abundant spawning salmon in the Squamish River. Their time here from November to February is a magnetic occasion for thousands of bird watchers and photographers, hoping to catch a glimpse or a shot of these beautiful creatures whose wing span can reach 2.5 metres, and whose flight speed can get up to 45 kilometres per hour.

The Squamish River in winter is enough of a draw itself for photographers and nature lovers, shown above at one of its narrowest points.

28

Squamish Harbour

Situated under impressive Mount Garibaldi, Squamish is a favourite sport destination of Vancouverites and tourists. Opportunities for activities as varied as hiking, mountain biking, golfing, fishing and rock climbing can be found here. Squamish also offers excellent water for kite-boarders and windsurfers, just off the Squamish Spit. Numerous organized activities can be observed and participated in, such as the Test of Metal Mountain Bike Race every June, the Squamish Triathlon and Sea to Sky Trail Ride in July and the Squamish Days Logger Sports in September.

Baynes Island

The Squamish River at Brackendale, Baynes Island and Mount Thyestes, the southeastern most peak of Tantalus Range.

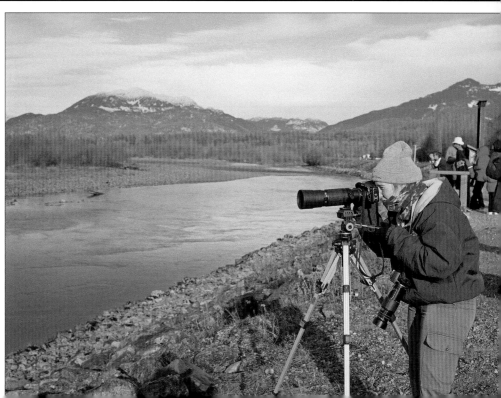

29

Squamish

Squamish Valley

The Outdoor Recreation Capital of Canada, as Squamish is often dubbed, is cradled by some of the most spectacular features of the British Columbian coast. The Coast Mountains and Garibaldi Provincial Park on one side, a view of Howe Sound on the other and the excellent four-lane connector to Vancouver and Whistler make Squamish one of the most popular and accessible places along the Sea to Sky corridor.

Adventure Centre

Important information about Squamish and the Sea to Sky corridor can be found at the Squamish Adventure Centre located in Squamish, just off the highway. If you need some local maps, brochures or are in the market for some mementos and gifts you can find them there.

30

Squamish

Tantalus Range

Rising above the Squamish River, as seen in the smaller picture, the Tantalus Range is a superb subject for photographers. Numerous alpine climbing routes for experienced climbers can be found and events such as the Tantalus Ridge Run are held every year. The heavily glaciated range, covering 306 square kilometres is located between the Ashlu and Squamish Rivers. Driving from Squamish to Whistler, the Tantalus Range follows on the left-hand side until the community of Garibaldi begins. The larger picture was taken from Round Mountain and shows the entire Tantalus Range with (from left) Omega Mountain, Mount Niobe, Alpha Mountain, Serratus Mountain, Mount Tantalus and Zenith Mountain.

31

Garibaldi Meadows

Hiking in Garibaldi Provincial Park is most popular in spring and summer, when wild flowers in full bloom spill down the hillsides. Gone are the heavy rains, the meadows are full of colour, the trees lush and green, and the sky a clear blue. This is the time to pack some hiking gear, grab a camera and hit the road! Garibaldi Provincial Park can thank the local climate for its numerous rich shades of green. Some parts of the park receive over 800 centimetres of rain or snow per year, because warm and moist air traveling from the ocean is blocked by the coastal mountains. The air then cools resulting in heavy precipitation, which feeds the western slopes of the park.

32

Mother of the Wind

Yes, the name 'Squamish' means 'Mother of the Wind' in the Coast Salish language. Another known name of the indigenous or First Nations people was 'Skwxwu7mesh', which means 'the people of sacred drinking water.' Where the Squamish River empties its waters into the Howe Sound, there is a world-renowned spot of water lovers, kite-surfers and windsurfers. Most days some 20 to 30 kite-surfers can be seen in the windy bay, accessed via the Squamish Spit.

Cleveland Avenue

Downtown Squamish along Cleveland Avenue, situated just beneath Diamond Peak.

33

Squamish

Alpha Mountain

A nighttime shot of Alpha Mountain during full moon, taken from Paradise Valley, near the Cheakamus River.

Serratus Mountain

Shown here to the right of Alpha Mountain, Serratus Mountain stands at 2,325 metres between Mount Tantalus and Lake Lovely Water. Uneven and rugged, the peak, like many other in the Tantalus Range, is mostly composed of loose rock.

Tantalus Range

Garibaldi Highlands

The town of Squamish is currently in the midst of a rapid expansion to the north. A popular new residential area near Squamish, Garibaldi Highlands, is pictured here.

Garibaldi Estates

The community that sits at the intersection of the Sea to Sky Highway and Garibaldi Way is Garibaldi Estates. New apartment buildings and townhouses are located near large department stores, supermarkets, hotels, construction suppliers, golf courses and more, bringing big-city services and conveniences to the country.

Raven's Plateau

The popular and expanding neighbourhood of Squamish, Raven's Plateau, is hidden within the valley created by the Stawamus Chief.

35

Squamish

Mamquam Mountain

Spring and summer colour the slopes of Garibaldi Provincial Park, as can be seen in this picture of Mamquam Mountain, as seen from the Diamond Head Trail. The overwhelmingly wide mountain stands like a backdrop wall to the valley.

Diamond Head Trail

Located south of Garibaldi Peak, a mountain with its spawning ice field can be seen from Squamish. This picture was taken from a hiking trail close to Mamquam Lake. After driving some 13 kilometres on the rough Garibaldi Park Road one can find the trailhead of the park's popular Diamond Head Trail.

36

Garibaldi Park

Diamond Head

The extinct volcano of Mount Garibaldi is the most visible landmark in this area. Located on the southern end of the mountain's Atwell Peak, Diamond Head (also known as Little Diamond Head), named for its sharp triangular apex, is the base for the south arête climb.

Mount Garibaldi

Pictured here is Mount Garibaldi as seen from the Diamond Head Trail. The massif was probably the first truly alpine peak in the Coast Mountain Range to be climbed. First sighted in 1860 by Captain George Henry Richards while navigating the waters of Howe Sound aboard the HMS Plumper, the mountain was named after Italian patriot Giuseppe Garibaldi by the same captain.

37

Garibaldi Park

Garibaldi Provincial Park

Mountains and glaciers, rivers, impressive forests and lakes, excellent conditions for skiers and hikers-this is Garibaldi Provincial Park, the southernmost part of the Coast Mountain Range. The park, dominated by 2,675 metre Mount Garibaldi, is made up of 1,958-square kilometres of wilderness and is forested by hemlock, fir, balsam and red cedar. Wildlife such as black and grizzly bears, mountain goats, deer and wolverines can be seen throughout the park. Aside from its diverse vegetation and wildlife, Garibaldi Provincial Park is also known for its great variety of mountains which make it attractive for hikers and nature photographers. Thanks to these attributes, the park has become a favourite getaway for tourists and local residents wishing to spend a weekend in the wild.

38

Rutherford River

Hidden deep in Garibaldi Provincial Park, the beautiful Rutherford River pictured here is not easily accessible. The bright sun shining on the day this shot was taken offered a unique dappling effect on the beautiful, but oft viewed scene.

Alice Lake

Family friendly Alice Lake, with a ninety site campground, is nestled near the Sea to Sky Highway, some 10 kilometres north of Squamish. The wide, clean shores of the lake make it a popular site for sunbathers as well as swimmers and campers.

39

Garibaldi Park

Mamquam River

Just a few kilometres after passing Squamish on the way to Whistler, turn right off Highway #99 just after the bridge, drive a few kilometers more until coming to a small parking lot and a golf course, and you will find yourself at the access of the Mamquam River, an excellent spot for year-round fly-fishing, including Coho and Pink salmon fishing in the fall.

Sea to Sky Golfing

The Sea to Sky area is popular not only for excellent hiking trails, breezy waters for windsurfing and creeks open for fly-fishing. Golfers, too, can find enjoyment on the many beautiful golf courses in Squamish, Furry Creek and Whistler. This picture shows the Golf and Country Club in Squamish, located by the Mamquam River.

40

Squamish

Paradise Valley

Turning left some 5 kilometres past Squamish, you will find beautiful forest scenes around Cheekye and Paradise Valley, like the example in this picture of the Cheakamus River in Paradise Valley.

Salmon Fishing

Salmon season opens in the area's most popular streams-the Squamish, Mamquam, and Cheakamus Rivers-towards the end of summer. These rivers offer excellent fishing, but with catch-and-release restrictions in some spots, so be sure to check out the local guidelines before heading out. Also remember that while the best time for salmon fishing is October and November, steelhead can be found in January and February.

41

Paradise Valley

Exodus Peak

A true outdoor experience lies in wait in the Squamish and Paradise Valleys, where the Elaho, Squamish and Cheakamus Rivers flow. Rustic campsites in wild settings or private sites along the rivers and creeks are favourite destinations of Vancouverites looking to escape big city distractions. Pictured here are Exodus Peak, a part of Pemberton Icefield and the Elaho River.

Mount Fee

The 2,162 metre peak of Mount Fee, as can be seen from the Squamish River Valley. The key features of the peak are the two sharp blades of volcanic rock jutting from its apex.

42

Squamish Valley

Ashlu Mountain

The granite peaks of Ashlu Mountain, located in the Ashlu-Elaho Divide, are 2,561 metres high. In the 1920s and 1930s mineral mining was prominent in the Ashlu Valley, however today it is an active logging site.

Zig Zag

The peak of Zig Zag, one of several peaks dominating the wild meadows of the Ashlu Valley, was photographed from a hiking trek to nearby Storey Peak.

43

Ashlu Mountain

Cheekye

Picture-perfect scenes are created by forests and woodlands throughout Paradise Valley. This picture was taken by the road to Evans Lake, home to a beautiful summer camp.

Seagram Creek

Seagram Creek flows from a small lake of the same name through the Squamish Valley before emptying into the Squamish River.

44

Paradise Valley

Brandywine Falls

Scenic attractions, including a fifteen-site campground, can be found along Brandywine Creek, which flows near Daisy Lake. A short walk from the parking lot near the Sea to Sky Highway, just eleven kilometers south of Whistler, will lead you to the viewpoint above, where the 66 metre high Brandywine Falls can be observed. Daisy Lake on the left side is also clearly visible. The second picture is of a nearby forest.

45

Black Tusk

The most photographed peak in Garibaldi Provincial Park, Black Tusk stands at 2,315 metres. The peak, made up of more than 200 metres of volcanic rock, resides near Garibaldi Lake. This peak also graces the cover of this book.

Zenith Mountain

The lunging, asymmetrical peak of Zenith Mountain rises above Tantalus Provincial Park at 1,980 metres. The heavily glaciated Tantalus Range, covering 306 square kilometres, is located between the Ashlu and Squamish Rivers and is a sub-range of the Pacific Ranges of the Coast Mountains.

46

Garibaldi Park

Mount Tantalus

The highest peak of the Tantalus Range is Mount Tantalus at 2,605 metres. The word 'tantalus,' which shares its root with the word 'tantalize,' is taken from the Greek myth about Tantalus, a man fated to serve his time in Hades half-submerged in cold water and taunted with fruit hanging just inches from his mouth.

Rubble Creek

Under Daisy Lake, near the Garibaldi-Black Tusk Trail, snow waters collect to create Rubble Creek. This trail is quite easy to find. Before Daisy Lake Dam turn right, walk about two kilometres to the parking lot, from where you can reach Garibaldi Lake in another eight kilometres. The peak of Black Tusk is a further eight kilometers down the trail.

Tantalus Range

Castle Towers Mountain

Castle Towers Mountain is at the centre of the picture above. Part of the Garibaldi Volcanic Belt, 'The Castle' is a 'lava spine': a cylindrical bulk of lava created by the compression of lava inside a volcanic vent. Just behind on the left is Mount Carr and on the right, Polemonium Ridge.

Upper Village

Upper Village in Whistler where Fairmont Chateau Whistler is nestled. Wizard Express and the Magic Chair lift skiers in minutes to 7th Heaven on Blackcomb, which, at 2,436 metres, is higher than the 2,181 metre Whistler Mountain.

Garibaldi Park

Metal Dome

Metal Dome Mountain was shot from Little Whistler Peak. The mountain is located on the line of the Brandywine Mountains. The sharp peak on the left is Pyroclastic and the large pyramid is Mount Cayley. Metal Dome, a large hill with gentle summits and slopes is ideal for skiing.

Welcome...

Welcome to the Whistler-Blackcomb Ski Resort, the most popular ski area in North America. Vancouver and Whistler will play host to the Olympic and Paralympic Winter Games in February 2010, marking the third time Canada has hosted the Olympic Games, after the 1976 Summer Games in Montreal and the Winter Olympics of 1988 in Alberta's Calgary.

49

Whistler

The Table

A feature of the Garibaldi Lake Volcanic Field, The Table is a flat-topped volcano which formed during the last ice-age when lava bubbled into the ice. The 2,021 metre Table attracts hundreds of hikers every summer.

Skiers

More than 60,000 skiers per hour can be propelled to the summits of Whistler and Blackcomb by way of 38 lifts, and the resort's annual snowfall of 10 metres ensures that kind of high ski traffic. Each mountain has over 100 runs, the two longest measuring 11 kilometres. Heli-skiing and boarding are popular options for thrill-seekers and cross-country skiers can enjoy Lost Lake, where 30 kilometres of scenic woodland tracks surround a glistening, icy lake.

Garibaldi Park

Empetrum Ridge

Little Whistler Peak with Harmony Express in the bottom left corner, Empetrum Ridge and Peak on the right the massif Black Tusk towering above it all. Black Tusk is a member of the Garibaldi Volcanic Belt, which was created when the Explorer Plate pushed underneath the Juan de Fuca Plate. The peak is a yearly destination for thousands of hikers, easily reached by several trails from Squamish and Whistler. Driving from Vancouver to Whistler, you will briefly see this peak several times, but don't try to stop along the road to take a picture-wait for the more satisfying views from Whistler.

Whistler Base

Skiers by Fitzsimmons Express in the Main Village.

51

Garibaldi Park

Mount Fissile

Overlord Glacier sits to the left of 2,439 metre Mount Fissile. The Oboe Summit, the lowest of the 'Musical Bumps' after Flute and Piccolo Summits, sits in the foreground.

Whistler at Christmas

Christmas decorations add sparkle and glitz to the nighttime view of Whistler's Town Plaza. Thanks to this twinkling night sky, a generous snowfall and the bustling energy of vacationing skiers, Whistler is a magical place to be during Christmas.

Garibaldi Park

Singing Pass

Singing Pass offers beautiful views of both the Spearhead and Fitzsimmons Ranges. In this picture, the Spearhead Range's Mount Trorey, Mount Pattison and Tremor Mountain stand to the left of Fitzsimmons Creek in the valley. The Singing Pass and its lower hills is on the right of this picture. Above the pass is Overlord Mountain and Mount Fissile.

Village Square

The Village Stroll, with its dense concentration of boutiques, restaurants and hotels leads to Village Square and the Town Plaza.

53

Whistler

Alta Lake

Like many features along the Sea to Sky Highway, Alta Lake holds a special place in Whistler's history. Enticed by stories of Whistler's immense beauty, Alex and Myrtle Philip moved to the area from Maine in 1911. After receiving confirmation of their original imaginings the couple decided to make the place their home and built the Rainbow Lodge in 1914 on the shores of Alta Lake, thereafter running the lodge for 34 years. Overlooking the Whistler Valley area from the peak of Whistler, one can take in views of Alta Lake beneath Mount Sproatt and the residential area of Alpine Meadows on the right.

Main Street

Townhouses near Main Street in Whistler village.

54

Whistler

Whistler Slopes

The Whistler Village Gondola connects Whistler Base and Main Village with Roundhouse Lodge. Fascinating views of the Whistler Valley and Spearhead Range can be observed from the ride, including prime views of Blackcomb Peak, Decker Mountain and Mount Trorey. Mount Currie, on the right, stands before the town of Pemberton, which was connected to Whistler by the Sea to Sky Highway in 1975.

Blackcomb Peak

A view of the Spearhead Range with Blackcomb Peak, Decker Mountain and Mount Trorey, from the Whistler Village Gondola. Aside from its several peaks, Spearhead Range is also made up of several glaciers.

55

Whistler

Whistler's Peak

The rocky peak of Whistler Mountain in the Fitzsimmons Range rises 2,181 metres above the town and resort of Whistler. Originally named London Mountain, the peak received its current name in 1966 with the opening of the resort. The new name was inspired was the whistling calls of the marmots living in burrows of the mountain. The smaller photo on this page depicts tourists enjoying the beauty of the peak.

Cheakamus Glacier

The small peak on the right of Castle Towers Mountain is the 2,590-metre Mount Carr. Under this peak is the ice-blue Cheakamus Glacier.

56

ILLANAAQ

Illanaaq the Inukshuk, which has been chosen as the logo of the 2010 Vancouver Winter Olympics, stands in stone on the peak of Whistler facing Black Tusk. Illanaaq is the Inuktitut word for 'friend'. An Inukshuk is a traditional stone marker which the Inuit used to guide their way across the treacherous Arctic. Whistler Peak can be reached in summer months using the Whistler Village Gondola to Roundhouse Lodge, however you can also hike the peak from the lodge or use open-air chair lift, which is pictured on the opposite page.

57

Garibaldi Park

Mount Davidson

Cheakamus Glacier stands in the centre of this mountain skyline. On its left is Mount Davidson stands opposite Castle Towers Mountain and the smaller peak of Mount Whirlwind stands to the left of Mount Davidson. For a little perspective, Castle Towers Mountain is approximately 3 kilometres from Mount Davidson, the highest point of which is exactly 12 kilometres from my camera.

Mountain Biking

BC's bikers love the terrain in Whistler, flocking to its trails as soon as the snows begin to melt in late April. Hundreds of available mountain bike trails add up to almost 250 kilometres, the most popular assortment found at Whistler Mountain Bike Park, accessible by Whistler Gondola and Fitzsimmons Chairs.

Cowboy Ridge

For adventurous skiers, try a backcountry day trip to the eastern outlier of Singing Pass, Cowboy Ridge.

Whistler Festivals

Concerts and festivals are year-round staples of life of Whistler. This picture was taken during the World Ski and Snowboard Festival, held every April at the base of Whistler Mountain, marking the end of the winter season. Raging for ten days and nights, the festival showcases live concerts, arts events, gear demos, pro ski and snowboard camps and all-night parties. Whistler's other popular events include the Children's Art Festival and the Kokanee Crankworx Mountain Bike Festival in July and the Music & Art Festival in August.

59

Whistler

Mount Currie

A strong telephoto lens was used for this unusual shot of the southwest side of Mount Currie, taken from Whistler Mountain. This mountain, located in the ridge above Pemberton just on the Garibaldi Provincial Park boundary stands roughly 25 kilometres before my camera. Mount Currie is also visible (the peak on the left) in the smaller picture on the next page.

Summer Trails

Hiking around Mount Garibaldi is very popular with hikers of all ages and skill levels. Well-maintained trails are accessible from five marked points between Squamish and Whistler. At Diamond Head there is a 34-bunk shelter for those wishing to make theirs an overnight trip.

60

Garibaldi Park

Wedge Mountain

This picture exemplifies the amazing views offered from the peak of Whistler. From left to right are Mount Weart, a small peak of Parkhurst Mountain and Wedge Mountain, the highest peak in Garibaldi Provincial Park at 2,891 metres.

Emerald Estates

Passing Whistler and heading to Pemberton, you will eventually drive alongside the lucid waters of Green Lake. Stop at the pull-off on your right before arriving at Emerald Estates and enjoy the views of the lake and of Blackcomb Mountain hovering in the distance. Wedgemount Glacier and Armchair Glacier can also be seen from this vantage point, making it an ideal stop for photographers.

61

Garibaldi Park

Whistler Aerial

The Whistler-Blackcomb Ski Resort, first opened in 1966 by Franz Wilhelmsen, quickly gained international fame and today is consistently rated the top ski resort in North America. The resort offers 12 Alpine bowls, over 200 marked trails and 38 lifts. Winter season is open from November to April on Whistler Mountain though summer skiing runs until July on Blackcomb. The opening of the resort inspired one of the earliest extensions of the Sea to Sky Highway, resulting in an extension from Horseshoe Bay to Whistler.

Whistler Village

Whistler, the municipality sitting at the foot of the resort, overflows with beautiful Alpine style hotels, lodges, eateries and recreational resorts, making time spent off the slopes as satisfying as time spent on.

Whistler

Green Lake

Green Lake, as mentioned previously, is located north of Whistler, alongside the Sea to Sky Highway. Several picnic spots dot the shores of the lake which always stays well-stocked with rainbow trout, dolly warden and sockeye salmon.

Whistler Living

Thanks to the numerous festivals already mentioned as well as golf courses, mountain bike and hiking trails and luxury establishments, Whistler is not only a popular getaway spot all year round, but also a much desired residential area.

63

Spearhead Range

Photographed from the peak of Whistler: Mount Trorey, Mount Pattison and the peaks of The Ripsaw, Mount Macbeth and Tremor Mountain, all part of the Spearhead Range.

Whistler Creekside

South of the main village of Whistler is Whistler Creekside, located at the base of the Dave Murray Downhill Run. Whistler Creekside is an ideal location for families in search of a quieter, homier mountain experience. With the Creekside Gondola connecting the village with Whistler Mountain, the spot is out of the way without being isolated. Of interest may be Franz's Trail Farmers Market every Saturday, offering fresh produce and displays of work by local artists.

64

Garibaldi Park

Mount Sproatt

Mount Sproatt, located in the Rainbow Mountains, taken from Whistler Mountain.

Whistler Town Plaza

In 1964, the Whistler Valley had no electricity, no roads and no running water. Two years later a four person gondola, chair-lift and a day lodge were constructed to accommodate the newly opened resort. In 1975, Whistler-Blackcomb was already famous across Canada and in 1977 the construction of the village began on some 50 acres of land. Shown here is the town plaza in Whistler Village as it appears today.

65

Whistler

Mount Weart

The second highest, but possibly the most beautiful peak in the park is Mount Weart, home to Armchair Glacier. The glacier, shooting out under the peaks of Mount Weart, is a favourite destination for helicopter tours and heli-skiing. The three-summitted massif can be seen perfectly from the shores of Green Lake.

Whistler Cay

The small private homes of Whistler Cay are located opposite Whistler Village on Highway #99. Alta Lake and the neighbourhood of Alta Vista are nearby.

Garibaldi Park

Whistler Mountain

Whistler Mountain from the vantage point of Blackcomb. The multi-summited peak of 2,181 metres, looms above Whistler Village in the Fitzsimmons Range, and can be reached by Whistler Village Gondola or Fitzsimmons Express. More chairlifts are found at the apex of the mountain, the newest of which will be the longest free-span lift in the world. The Peak to Peak Gondola will be opened in December 2008 and will boast a total length of 4.4 kilometres and will be as high as 415 metres above the valley floor.

The smaller picture was taken at the Whistler Base, where Excalibur Gondola to Blackcomb and Fitzsimmons Express and Whistler Village Gondola to Whistler operate.

67

Whistler

Blackcomb Mountain

Blackcomb Mountain claims over 3,400 acres of ski-able terrain, 12 alpine bowls, 3 glaciers, 17 lifts and over 100 marked runs; the longest running 11 kilometres. Blackcomb Mountain was first opened for skiers in 1980, when the conflation of Whistler and Blackcomb made it the largest ski area in North America.

7th Heaven

Skiers on Blackcomb Peak headed for 7th Heaven.

Garibaldi Lake

A deep, sub-alpine basin, Garibaldi Lake's geological surroundings were formed almost entirely by volcanic activity. Almost completely enclosed by mountains, both volcanic and not, the lake was blocked by lava from Mount Price and Clinker Peak which dammed its water behind a formation called The Barrier. The turquoise water of the lake is due to meltwater from the Sphinx and Sentinel Glaciers. This area is well-known among hikers and nature photographers, for whom there are two shelters and several tent sites. Several lakes and streams offer good fishing, though access tends to be difficult, making the area ideal for the more adventurous fisherman.

Alpine Meadows

A neighbourhood of Whistler near Green Lake, known for its excellent cross-country ski trails.

69

Garibaldi Park

Mount Moe

Mystery Glacier, Mount Moe and Mount Cook taken from between Pemberton and Whistler.

Roundhouse Lodge

The area surrounding the Roundhouse Lodge, the terminus of the Whistler Village Gondola, is always a busy place. Panoramic views can be enjoyed by skiers and visitors alike. The small panoramic picture on the opposite page overlooks the whole area as seen from the Roundhouse Lodge.

Cinder Cone

From left - Castle Towers Mountain, Helm Peak, Cinder Cone (at centre) and Black Tusk reaching into the clouds. Small Corrie Lake lies beneath Cinder Cone. Garibaldi Lake lies hidden beneath the skyline. Gentian Ridge is just left of Cinder Cone.

Coast Mountains

The Coast Mountains make up the western range of the North American Mainland Cordillera covering most of British Columbia's coast. The range, starting in Yukon and ending near the Fraser Valley, is 1,620 kilometres long and 190 kilometres wide. Mount Waddington, at 4,019 metres, is the highest peak of the range (not pictured here), and is located in the Pacific Ranges, close to Tatla Lake.

71

Whistler

Pemberton

Over the course of millions of years, the Lillooet River brought rich soil to the Pemberton Valley, resulting in a green pocket of agricultural land, widely known for its potatoes. Affectionately termed 'Spud Valley,' Pemberton Valley is famous for its 'seed potatoes' which it has produced since 1967, making it the first commercial seed potato area in the world. The rustic village was named for Joseph Despard Pemberton, a surveyor-general for the Hudson Bay Company. In 1914 the extension of the railway line to Pemberton brought more families to settle in the valley. The highway to Whistler was finally pushed through in 1975 and the connection with the lower mainland was fully opened. Operated by the Archives Society and Pemberton Museum, a collection of two historic homes and artifacts documents the local history before the arrival of Europeans. The museum and gift shop with a charming assortment of locally crafted gifts is open from June to September. One can also find a historic hotel, golf courses, camp sites, motels and much more in Pemberton.

72

Green River

The Green River floats through Narin Falls Provincial Park, and over Narin Falls. The river then empties into Lillooet Lake, which brought the first settlers to Pemberton in 1890. This view of the river is from a trail in the local campground. The second picture is of nearby Narin Falls.

Narin Falls

A short distance from Pemberton, the area surrounding Narin Falls and the Green River offer a truly natural experience. The easy hiking trail along the Green River is an easy family walk which will place you in the centre of pristine wilderness.

73

Joffre Peak

Joffre Peak, situated 20 kilometres south of Pemberton, can be seen from the spot where Duffey Lake Road passes through Cayoosh Pass. To the left of snowy Joffre Peak is Mount Matier. The small mountain peeking out between the purple wildflowers in the center of the photo is Vantage Peak.

Lillooet Lake

Popular for its many rustic campsites as well as for fishing, Lillooet Lake is visited by hundreds every week. The lake is located east of Pemberton. A rough logging road along the lake runs to Port Douglas by Harrison Lake.

Stein Valley

Mount Currie

The massive, multi-summited Mount Currie covered in snow. The north side, facing Pemberton is 2,100 metres high. Salish First Nations People were the first who settled at the foot of this mountain near D'Arcy, however, the mountain was named after Scotsman John Currie, the first permanent non-native settler in the area, whose ranch was just at the mountain's base.

Cayoosh Range

Hundreds of beautiful scenic points will pique your curiosity along the route from Pemberton to Lillooet. You will witness the force of nature in action as rivers, mountains and lakes rush, flow and rise around you. You may easily become entranced enough to stay overnight in some of the quiet, private campsites along the road.

Pemberton

Stein Valley

Joffre Lake Provincial Park and Stein Valley Provincial Park are accessible along the way from Pemberton to Lillooet.

Duffey Lake Provincial Park

Alpine views can be seen just by driving along the famously twisty Duffey Lake Road from Pemberton to Lillooet. Some of the mountains are over 2,900 metres high. Joffre Peak is 2,721 metres, Mount Rohr 2,423 metres, Cayoosh Mountain 2,561 metres, Skihist Mountain 2,968 metres and Mount Brew located close to Lillooet reaches 2,891metres. Duffey Lake Provincial Park spreads out across 2,379 hectares and was established in 1993.

Joffre Lake

If driving along Duffey Lake Road from Pemberton heading to Lillooet heats up your engine, take a break and walk around the magnificently coloured Lower Joffre Lake. You will see the glacier-laden peaks of the Joffre Glacier Group steeply rising above, and can hike along 11 kilometre trails in two directions leading to Middle Joffre Lake and Upper Joffre Lake. By the time you return to your car you will undoubtedly feel rejuvenated enough to continue on your journey.

Mount Matier

Possibly the most picturesque spot along Duffey Lake Road is the tail-end of the road, with views of Mount Brew, colourful Cayoosh Creek and Seton Lake.

77

Duffey Road

Cayoosh Creek

Cayoosh Creek, near Seton Lake, in autumn.

Duffey Lake

The popular Duffey Lake located halfway along Duffey Lake Road.

Seton Lake

Seton Lake, pictured on the next page is located in the Seton Ridge, almost at the end of the Sea to Sky Highway, near Lillooet. The lake is popular for family outings and trout fishing, and a salmon hatchery is located on the spawning channel right by the lake.

Duffey Road

Seton Ridge

Seton Ridge surrounds the final segment of Duffey Lake Road. The picture here was taken just before Lillooet. The road passes beautiful scenery and a large difference of elevation.

This book covers the area from Vancouver to Seton Lake. Our other book, <u>Fraser Valley</u>, continues the journey through the area via Highway #12 from Lillooet to Hope, Highway #1 from Chilliwack and then along the Fraser River to Abbotsford, Mission, Fort Langley and back to Vancouver. Imagine the highways as an ellipse, the top arc being Lillooet and the bottom arc, Vancouver. The left side of this ellipse is covered in <u>Sea To Sky</u>, while the right side of the ellipse is photographed in <u>Fraser Valley</u>.

Lillooet

Across Labrador, Newfoundland

Josef M. Hanus with the Coast Mountains in the background

Across Liard River, NWT and in Yukon, below

Travels through Canada...

My first cross-country trip across Canada in 1999 completely changed my business orientation. In what I had thought was a one-time deal, I traveled some 30,000 kilometres across this beautiful country I have called my home since 1985, with my brother John. The trip took us three months in all and left us a bit overwhelmed, and more than a little bit tired, not having had much experience taking pictures while driving great distances over such a long period of time. Prior to this trip I had published two similar books, Vancouver and British Columbia, which, since I live in Vancouver, had not required such long-distance travel.

Returning home, just before entering British Columbia, I breathed a sigh of relief at the thought that I would never again undertake such a lengthy and exhausting trip. However, as I pulled into the driveway of my house, closing the curtain on our journey, I had a sudden change of heart. Even before I turned off the engine, I found myself planning another trip. Despite the diligence and energy required by such a trip, I was determined to travel cross-country the following year, though, the next time, I had decided, my family would come along for the ride.

After proposing my plan, I asked my wife and son their thoughts. They laughed and told me I was crazy and that it was too early to think about another trip. They soon saw, however, how determined I was. The following spring the book resulting from the trip, Canada, was published and became very popular, and, taking my good fortune as a sign, I took my son Josef along to photograph the Northwest Territory, Yukon and Alaska in May of 2000.

For my third cross-country trip in 2001 I also traveled with my son, who had by this time become my business partner, and over the next several years we made many more trips, varying from localized trips across British Columbia for our new issue of British Columbia, to longer trips focusing on the Rockies and Prairies, even traveling as far as Southern Ontario and Toronto.

Aside from altering my business orientation, traveling throughout Canada has truly affected my sense of scale. An example of a short trip now is from Vancouver to the Rockies and back, about 3,000 kilometres. Medium distanced trips are now to the Prairies or Toronto, a long trip goes further east to Atlantic Canada, and an "extra-long" trip means Newfoundland and Labrador, some thirty thousand kilometres round-trip. These distances are not, of course, the most direct routes across Canada, for, while taking pictures, we constantly travel back and forth, to the north and south, east and west, constantly stopping over and switching back in order to produce the best photographs possible.

Despite becoming hooked on long-distance travel, I had already radically reduced my ideas regarding world travel and decided to spend almost all of my time in Canada, having become enamored with this majestic county after numerous trips across British Columbia. I bought a strong diesel truck, which, along with my camper, proved to be an excellent investment, allowing me and my son to travel comfortably and safely around the country. Each trip inspires new ideas for new books. After the first trip across the country, for example, I flew to the Yukon to take more autumn pictures to incorporate into Canada. It was my awe of the beauty of the northernmost part of Canada that inspired my subsequent trip with my son. When we prepared British Columbia for printing, we realized that it wasn't possible to show the beauty of this province in one single book, so we decided to publish four local titles covering British Columbia and two more titles from Ontario, Southern Ontario and Toronto. Considering the size and undiscovered treasures hiding around every corner of this country, our readers can expect many more installations in our Canadian series.

Photographer and Publisher

Author, photographer and owner of JH Fine Art Photo Ltd., Josef Hanus is one of the most accredited and celebrated scenic and wilderness photographers in North America. He has created and published over 150 titles of Canadian calendars using only his work since 1989. He is now working on a series of travel-photographic books with the theme closest to his heart: Canada. As of 2008 he will have self-published 16 books, all of which have become best-sellers in their category. His award-winning photographs and best-selling Canadian calendars and photographic books have arisen purely out of hard work and a strong commitment to the subject matter.

After graduating from an art and photography institute in Prague, Czech Republic, Josef began his career working for magazines and newspapers, and has had tens of thousands of photographs and articles published throughout Europe and North America. Though he has photographed a variety of subjects, observing nature through his lens has remained his greatest love. The careful study of objects trained his taste and aptitude for scenic views and his eye to the height of artistic professionalism. But his sensitive sight is not the only source of success. Over the years, he has perfectly selected his professional partners, including his son Josef with whom he has worked since 1997, and has patiently tested various types of cameras and lenses for his high quality work. The result of these efforts can be seen in his products, though that is not all. People love Josef's photographic books and calendars, because Josef loves to create them. This care is consistently evident in each tiny detail.

 About the Heart: JH Fine Art Photo's published products are visibly marked with their trademark, Canada's maple leaf enveloped with a red heart. The company logo was beautifully re-designed in 3D by Jan Hanus, who joined the company in 2007.